Modern Egypt and Its Heritage

Modern Egypt and Its Heritage

Carolyn Fluehr-Lobban
Rhode Island College

The Carnegie Museum of Natural History

This publication was made possible through a grant from the National Endowment for the Humanities, a federal agency.

Published by The Carnegie Museum of Natural History, Pittsburgh, PA 15213

Manufactured in the United States of America

ISBN *0-911239-13-8*
Library of Congress Catalog Card Number: 89-85820

Front cover drawing: detail of inlaid panel with design representative of Islamic art found in Egypt.

Contents

About the Author

Carolyn Fluehr-Lobban is a Philadelphia native trained in anthropology, with bachelor's and master's degrees from Temple University and a doctorate from Northwestern University. Since 1970 she has spent four years conducting research in the Nile Valley, including both the Sudan and Egypt. During 1982–83 she was a fellow at the American Research Center in Egypt while studying Egyptian family law. Her book, *Islamic Law and Society in the Sudan*, was published in 1987 in London by Frank Cass, Ltd. She is currently professor of anthropology and coordinator of international education at Rhode Island College in Providence, Rhode Island.

It is ironic to the cultural anthropologist that Egypt is better known for its antiquities than for its rich and fascinating face today. This is perhaps a result of Europe's historical fascination with the wonders of ancient Egypt stemming from the time of Herodotus, when Egypt was already an old empire. Certainly this interest extends to the time of the Napoleonic occupation at the close of the eighteenth century, when the European study of "the East" focused on Egypt. Even today tourists flock to the Nile Valley to view the monuments left by the ancients but appear to have little interest in the historical treasures of Islam or the contemporary lives of Egyptian rural and urban dwellers, who now make up the most populous nation in the Middle East with Africa's largest city, Cairo. This booklet introduces the richness of contemporary Egypt, beginning, of course, with its complex historical background.

Culture Shaped by History: Pharaonic, Islamic, European Colonial

Egyptians are proud to announce to the foreign visitor that their country is the Mother of the World *(al-Umm al-Donia)* because of the grandeur of its ancient civilization and its great cultural contributions to the world. To the untutored visitor this may appear boastful; however, closer study reveals that Pharaonic culture contributed seminally to the religion, art, architecture, medicine, and philosophy of Western culture, making Egypt one of the world's great "Mothers" or centers of ancient civilization.

By about 5000 B.C. predynastic Egyptians had established farming communities in the Nile Valley, supplementing their diet by hunting and gathering. They based their agriculture on the Mesopotamian domesticates, borrowing that region's sheep, goats, wheat, and barley complex. At least two millennia of agricultural life preceded the origin of the unified state that signaled the beginning of dynastic Egypt around 3100 B.C. The thirty-one dynasties that followed until the fourth century B.C. represent one of the most continuous political orders in human history, a monument to ancient Egyptian governmental structure, religion, and socioeconomic organization. A remarkable legacy of monuments and texts has been left to us to study, and increasingly archaeologists and anthropologists are turning their attention toward the daily lives of everyday people in ancient Egypt. It is through their efforts that we are able to comprehend the remarkable continuity, especially of farming practices and house styles, that has characterized adaptation to life in the Nile Valley.

The great efflorescence of Egyptian culture throughout the dynastic period presents us with stunning art and architectural achievements, such as the pyramids, and also with great cultural contributions in the realm of ideas—of science, mathematics, and philosophy—many of which are still with us today. Religious concepts of death and rebirth, the afterlife, and immortality of the soul are Egyptian innovations that very likely can be traced as contributing to the three great monotheistic religions in the Middle East—Judaism, Christianity, and Islam. Indeed, some scholars make the case that monotheism itself may have had

The pyramids and sphinx at Giza are towering reminders of the Pharaonic Period, the first major influence in shaping modern Egypt.

its first impulses in Egypt at the time of Pharaoh Amenhotep IV (Akhenaten, New Kingdom, ca. 1352–36 B.C.) with the worship of the sun god, Aten. Certain mythological themes that have been common to Western culture, such as fratricidal strife in the beginnings of human society and birth-rebirth cycles, predate their European appearance by millennia in ancient Egypt.

Ultimately, the Ptolemaic-Roman[1] occupation of Egypt at the end of the dynastic period provided the bridge that linked the Pharaonic Egyptian and European cultures. At this time Egypt was already an

1. "Ptolemaic" refers to the dynasty that ruled Egypt from about 332 to 30 B.C., after its conquest by Alexander the Great. During this period Egypt was under Greek and Macedonian political rule. At the same time Egyptian cultural influence spread to Europe.

ancient state in a period of decline, while the Macedonian, Greek, and Roman societies were entering a period of ascendancy. Encountering the magnitude and depth of Egyptian culture must have been a powerful experience for the European conquerors. A strong argument can be made that the Greeks copied the Pharaonic temple construction when designing their fluted columns, lintels, and hypostyle halls. This classical "Greek" architecture has spread its influence to the New World and can best be seen today in the United States in Washington, D.C. A striking example is the Washington Monument, which imitates an Egyptian obelisk.

With the occupation of Egypt, first by the Ptolemaic kings and subsequently by the Romans, Pharaonic culture was slowly extinguished, although the Coptic (Christian) community did preserve and transmit the remains of the ancient Egyptian language. When in the seventh century A.D. the Arabs with their religion of Islam penetrated Egypt, their rich new culture built on the remnants of the Ptolemaic and Roman cultures. As Arab Muslims settled in Egypt, they established a new city at Fustat that laid the foundation for Cairo, making it the longest continuously inhabited city in the world, having passed its first millennium. With Arab settlement also came the Arabic language, which today is the official language of the country, spoken by Christian and Muslim alike. A succession of Muslim rulers, beginning with the Fatamids (A.D. 969–1171), governed Egypt, with each empire leaving behind its distinctive architectural style preserved to this day in a rich array of mosques found throughout the old city of Cairo. Many of these, such as the Al-Azhar, the mosque of Qait Bey, Ibn Tulun, Sultan Hassan, and Mohammed Ali, are such perfect visible

The Mohammed Ali mosque in Cairo is a symbol of the rich Islamic culture, the second significant influence in molding modern Egypt.

relics of the glories of the Islamic empires that they are treasured throughout the Middle East and Islamic world.

When in 1517 Ottoman Turks overturned the Mamluks, who had ruled Egypt since 1250, Egypt became an overseas province of Turkey and one of its most prized possessions. Egypt subsequently endured four centuries of Turkish occupation. However, it was during this period that many of the basic institutions that have shaped modern Egyptian life—government, law, municipal service, land registration, tenure, and taxation—were put into place. Under the Sultan Mohammed Ali (beginning in 1805) an all-Egyptian army was created, lands confiscated by the Mamluks were reallocated to the peasantry, and the modern cash crop, cotton, was developed. Under the Khedive Ismail, a descendant of Mohammed Ali, the Suez Canal was opened in 1869, placing Egypt in a central, strategic position in relationship to Europe and making it all the more attractive to developing imperial interests in Europe.

During Turkish rule there was a brief French adventure in Egypt under Napoleon (1798–1802), a prelude to a later, more aggressive European expansion. Beginning with this encounter, the French language and culture, especially through the introduction of the Napoleonic Code in law, have had a profound and lasting effect on modern Egypt. However, the most influential European power has been England, which established a protectorate in 1882 as the rule of khedives was waning. The English subsequently governed Egypt indirectly until 1952, ruling the country in the name of the Egyptian King Farouq. The English built their own administrative structure upon the Ottoman base and developed Egyptian cotton for the British textile industry and the international market, while reaping the benefits of their control of international shipping through the Suez Canal.

England's colonial presence generated an anticolonial movement among the Egyptian intelligentsia and government workers, who began to forge a nationalist movement that presented its demand for Egyptian independence for the first time in 1918. The famous Wafd delegation, formed at this time, spoke not only against British rule but for independence that had not existed in Egypt since the demise of Pharaonic civilization. The nationalist movement expanded throughout the decades of the first half of the twentieth century and culminated in the Egyptian 1952 Revolution, when the Free Officers Movement under Gamal Abdel Nasser

The old Shepherd's Hotel in Cairo, shown in this early twentieth-century photograph, is representative of the European influence during Egypt's colonial period.

forced King Farouq to abdicate the throne, thus ending English control. Nasser ruled Egypt until his death in 1970 and became a revered patriot as well as a beloved leader of the Arab world and the Third World generally, because of his significant leadership in the Arab nationalist and nonaligned movements. Thus, Egypt entered the modern world as an independent nation-state.

Egypt as a Crossroads Between the Middle East, Africa, and Europe

Egypt's location as the keystone region at the center of the Afro-Asian geographical nexus is apparent from ancient times. During periods of conquest in ancient Egypt, both by foreign invaders and by Egyptians attacking Near Eastern states, the ancient Egyptians and the peoples of Syro-Palestine were introduced to each other's culture. The ancient Egyptians also came into contact with the Nubians to the south and the Libyans to the west through their continued struggle to protect their borders and expand their sources of raw materials. The Ptolemaic and Roman periods brought additional contact with Mediterranean countries.

The concept of Egypt as a crossroads between the Middle East, Africa, and Europe did not actually take root, however, until the period of the great expansion of Islam in the seventh and eighth centuries A.D. At this time Egypt served as a bridge for the spread of the Muslim faith, first into North Africa and then, with the Moorish occupation of the Iberian Peninsula, from northwest Africa into Europe.

During colonial times both the French and British viewed Cairo as the entryway to the rest of the African continent and to many of the colonial outposts in the Middle East. Cairo was and still is a communications hub, a necessary first stop before journeying into the interior of Africa or the Muslim lands of southwest Asia. After independence Nasser's political philosophy of linkage was symbolized in his active support for Afro-Asian solidarity movements.

The ancient Egyptians came into contact with the cultures of nearby regions. This drawing, copied from a painted scene in the tomb of Sety I, shows (from left) individuals from Egypt, Syro-Palestine, Nubia, and Libya.

Egypt's proximity to Europe should not be overlooked; nor should its history of political and cultural relationships with European countries dating from Ptolemaic-Roman times to the end of British colonialism. In addition to its political history, Egypt has had a special connection with the peoples of southern Europe, especially apparent today in the sizeable Greek community found in Alexandria and as a merchant group throughout Egypt.

Obviously flowing from the rich history of contacts among the peoples of Asia, Africa, and Europe has been an equally rich blending of cultural and physical types. In New Kingdom times of Pharaonic Egypt the only culture the ancient Egyptians recognized was

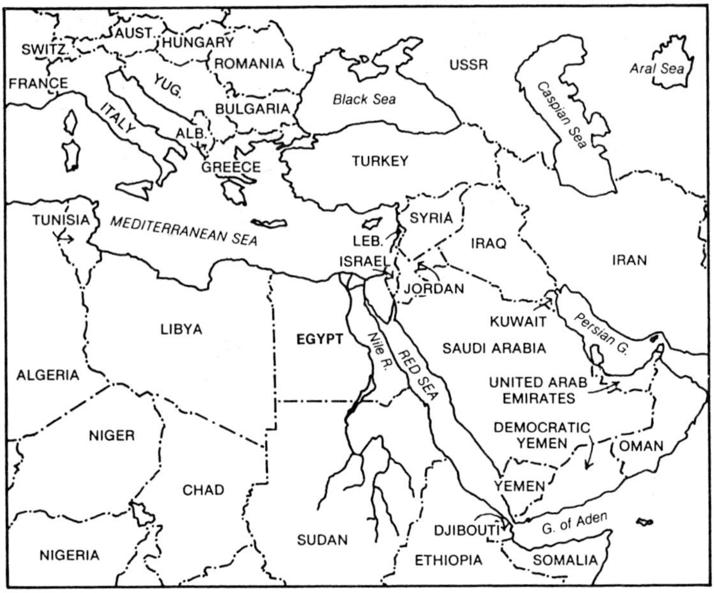

Since earliest times Egypt has been the center of the Afro-Asian geographical connection. With the expansion of the Islamic period, it became the crossroads between the Middle East, Africa, and Europe. This map shows modern Egypt's strategic position.

Egyptians show great physical diversity (clockwise from top left): Nubian man from Aswan, young girl from a rural area in the Delta region, a government official from Cairo, and a Nubian man residing in Cairo.

Egyptian; therefore, any person who was a member of another cultural group, that is, Nubians, Libyans, or Syro-Palestines, could become Egyptian by practicing Egyptian culture and speaking the Egyptian language. That slow integration formed the basis of today's physical and cultural blend. Over the millennia, from Ptolemaic-Roman times on, contact and mingling with these peoples increased, creating a truly multiracial and, to a lesser extent, multicultural situation in Egypt. Walking the streets of Cairo or Alexandria, one sees faces showing a mixture of features that can best be described as Afro-Arab or Afro-Asiatic. Lighter skin tones gradually grade into relatively darker shades of brown as one moves south along the Nile River. Variations in dress, dialectical changes in spoken Arabic, and the persistence of Nubian languages are evidence of cultural autonomy and differences in the contemporary Egyptian state; but overriding Egyptian nationality binds all of these people together.

Major Features Shaping Egyptian Society

With all the richness and variety of the Egyptian historical and cultural experience, there are certain key internal forces that form the foundations of modern Egyptian society. The first, and most basic, is the significance of the Nile River and the bond that Egyptians have to the land and to agrarian life. As obvious as this may seem, it is the most fundamental aspect of Egyptian life, so basic that it in-

Egyptian artists are often inspired to portray the fellaheen. *Pieces like these can be found for sale throughout Egypt.*

spires its own poets, artists, and intellectuals to see the truest representation of the Egyptian people in the *fellaheen*, the farmers of old, the peasants of today. Farming methods in the Nile Valley showed an amazing persistence from ancient times to the construction of the dams on the river, with little need for change given the regularity of the annual flood and the rich alluvial soil deposited each year. The irrigation technique of lifting water with *shadufs* (well-sweeps with a counterbalance) is depicted in Pharaonic scenes and continued into the twentieth century until the impact of the High Dam at Aswan was felt. Today, because of the dams, instead of a single annual crop, an astonishing three crops per year can be produced. Despite this technical advance, Egypt is not self-sufficient in food

Two men pull a wooden plow while two others guide the implement in this relief from the tomb of Paheri, early Dynasty XVIII (ca. 1539-1425 B.C.), at El-Kab.

Although mechanized farming is increasing, traditional agricultural techniques, such as the shaduf *and wooden plows, still prevail throughout Egypt, demonstrating continuity with the past. Here a young boy supervises a water buffalo that is turning a Persian waterwheel in a field near Zagazig.*

production and must import grain from the United States to meet its daily bread requirements. The problem is multifaceted, involving not only insufficient land and water, but also an increasingly impoverished peasantry, a large percentage of whom have had to migrate to the cities or abroad for wage labor. This is Egypt's great tragedy today.

The second major feature shaping Egyptian life is the religion of Islam. Egypt's dominantly Muslim population belongs to the great Sunni branch of Islam as opposed to the Shi'a minority found in Iran, Iraq, and in lesser numbers elsewhere in the Middle East and Asia. Sunni Muslims make up the vast majority of the world's estimated eight hundred million to one billion Muslims. The difference between Shi'a and Sunni Islam is not doctrinal but stems from their disagreement over who succeeded as head of the Muslim community after the death of Mohammed.

Egypt is home to Al-Azhar University, which is internationally recognized as the major center of Islamic learning. Like Cairo, this university has passed its one-thousandth anniversary, making it the oldest continuous university in the world.

Because of Egypt's history and huge Muslim population, what occurs within Egyptian Islam is followed closely outside of Egypt. This has been especially apparent in the recent period following the Islamic revolution in Iran, with the question "Is Egypt also ripe for an Islamic revolution?" frequently posed after the assassination of Anwar Sadat in 1981 by a militant Islamic organization.

Not since the overarching, powerful unity of the Pharaonic state has anything had such an effect on Egyptian culture as the religion of Islam. The community of believing Muslims, the *Umma*, represents a powerful force for unity, bringing together rural and urban, Upper and Lower Egypt into the brotherhood of Islam. This strength has international implications as well. Small wonder that the struggle against Zionism and the state of Israel has been couched in terms of *jihad* or holy war. It is also interesting to note that although one might expect an internal Muslim-Christian conflict, the Coptic Christian minority, between 6 and 8 percent of the population, has an exemplary history of nationalist and patriotic activity.

Like any other religious group, Egyptian Muslims do not constitute a homogeneous body, in terms of either thought or practice. Many people are Muslim in little more than name or family origin, while others practice the fundamentals of the religion without any commitment to activism. A growing minority, however, are dedicated to the growth of the influence of Islam in government, law, and social affairs. The politically organized Muslim Brotherhood and its offshoots in the Islamic revival or fundamentalist movements have been active throughout the twentieth century and especially in the last decade, using tactics of public demonstrations and electoral politics to implement their agenda for Islamic reform. New religious and social organizations, offering a variety of health and human services at lower cost based on Islamic organizational principles, have become very popular alternatives to government facilities. Islamic banks, using principles of mutual investment rather than the forbidden interest taking, are a growing alternative to Egyptian national and Western banks.

One obvious change has been the shift over the past decade from a majority of women wearing Western-style dress to a majority adopting a revived form of Islamic dress. Egyptian Islamic dress has a distinc-

The tombs of local saints in rural Egypt are central to the beliefs of popular Islam and religious folk tradition.

Many Egyptian women are choosing to wear a revived style of Islamic dress, instead of Western-derived fashions.

tive and very fashionable style of its own, with long dresses, long-sleeved blouses, and a variety of attractive head coverings. This quiet revolution, especially among young, urban, and educated women, is only one indication of the increased influence of Islamic values noticeable in Egypt today.

The Rural-Urban Continuum

Although Egypt has been and still is the Gift of the Nile, and although the rural, agrarian *fellaheen* represent the heart and soul of Egypt, the pace of urbanization has been phenomenal, resulting in basic social change. Today the rural-urban ratio of Egypt's fifty million people still tilts slightly toward the rural side, with 55 percent of Egyptians residing in the countryside. However, 45 percent of the population is urban, and the rapid migration over the past several decades is straining Egypt's cities. Cairo's population alone has grown from approximately three million at the time of independence in 1952 to a staggering eleven to fifteen million today. The influence of Cairo extends beyond its being Egypt's paramount city in every respect to its being the intellectual and cultural capital of the Middle East.

Connecting both urban and rural Egypt, the Nile is the lifeblood of this dominantly desert country. Apart from the few Bedouin inhabiting the arid lands, the vast majority of the Egyptian population live in densely populated villages, towns, and cities along the river and in the Delta. Settlement is so thick on the banks of the Nile that it is often difficult to determine where the

Automobiles lining streets are only one sign of the rapid change affecting Egypt's villages. One can also find, for example, stores selling televisions and other appliances, traffic jams, and railroad lines running through town.

rural ends and urban begins. Many towns with populations in the hundreds of thousands resemble small cities, while Egypt's urban centers are so crowded with rural migrants that some areas take on village-like characteristics. Rural women clad in long, flowing black dresses *(gellabiyas)* with colorful head scarves and rural men in *gellabiyas* and turbans are common sights in the major urban centers, making up a new population of "rurbanites" (Abu-Lughod, 1971:187).

Cairo's poorest neighborhoods are regionally diverse and overcrowded, but this particular combination of

Rural folk are ever-present in the city of Cairo.

poverty and crowded housing conditions has not resulted in the high rates of crime that have afflicted our crowded U.S. cities. Most probably the explanation for this is the continuing strength of the extended family, which makes neighborhoods communities rather than anonymous agglomerations of people. Middle-class urbanites enjoy larger flats and a better standard of living, but even these long-term urban residents maintain frequent contact with the rural village of their origin. Many retain landholdings and operating farms, which they direct from the city.

In the world revolution of mass communications, Egypt has been a pacesetter for the Third World, with a massive penetration of radio and television into the rural areas. Virtually every rural household either owns a TV or has access to one in the community, and much of the programming is Egyptian in origin, rather than being dependent on canned imports from the West so characteristic of other non-Western nations. Rural peoples can, therefore, be in touch with major events of the day through the media or through contact with their relatives who have migrated to the city.

For the past two decades, in addition to the migration to the cities, there has been a massive out-migration abroad, especially to the oil-producing countries, for better wages. The remunerations sent homc have been a boost to the Egyptian economy, but the 1987 decline in oil prices has caused many of the estimated two to three million Egyptians working abroad to return home to a limited economic future.

Family Life and the Status of Women

Family relationships are at the basis of every Egyptian's identity, and family ties are at the core of every Egyptian's life. To say that kinship is organized along patrilineal extended family lines does not really capture the meaning and significance of the role of the family in Egypt, indeed, throughout the Middle East. The extended family represents both genealogical and physical closeness in rural Egypt because close kin not only are related by blood and marriage but also are one another's closest neighbors or even co-residents of a single house. Even in urban Egypt extended family patterns have not broken down, and large families may occupy several adjacent flats or several stories of a single building. Family origin determines to a very great extent one's occupation in life as well as one's marriage partner. Marriage of cousins is strongly preferred and statistically the most frequent type, with the father's brother's daughter being the traditional favored choice for a spouse. Cousin marriage is understood as a means of consolidating family wealth as well as affording greater security and protection for the woman in marriage.

Patrilineal extended families with high rates of cousin marriage are characteristic of all Egyptian life, but the regulation of family affairs differs on religious grounds between Muslims and Christians. Polygyny is permitted in Islam, although only a very small percentage of Egyptian men actually take a second wife, largely because of the substantial dower that must be paid to the wife and the subsequent maintenance costs. Divorce is allowed in Islam but forbidden in Cop-

The author's husband and daughter pose with an extended family in Maadi, a suburb of Cairo.

tic Christianity. Traditionally, the Muslim husband has had the unilateral right of divorce, but twentieth-century reforms have lessened his power over the wife and have increased her grounds for obtaining a judicial divorce. The divorce rate in Egypt's cities is about half that of the United States, with about one in four marriages—usually the riskier unions with nonrelatives—ending in divorce. Recent reforms have placed certain constraints on husbands. For example, if a man takes more than one wife, he must obtain the first wife's consent before he marries a second time. And if a man divorces a wife with children, the mother is allotted the house and apartment and under certain conditions can retain custody of her children for an increased period of time.

About 25 percent of the Egyptian work force is female, according to official statistics; however, a very large number of women are involved in the infor-

These urban women, participating in an Egyptian Day celebration at Cairo American College, show some of the diversity of women's dress found in Egypt today.

mal sector as small-scale entrepreneurs, domestics, or other low-skill jobs, in addition to their household and domestic chores. This official statistic reflects one of the highest rates of female employment in the Middle East. Education for girls, which historically has lagged behind that for boys, has just about caught up in the urban areas. A fair measure of this equalization is Cairo University's enrollment of about 50,000 students, approximately 50 percent of which is female. Many women have entered the medical, legal, and engineering professions in addition to the more typical careers of teaching and nursing. Women have also been elected to Parliament and served as government ministers and as ambassadors representing their country abroad.

The feminist movement in Egypt dates to the time of the earliest nationalist demonstrations during the 1919–24 period, when veiled women marched with male compatriots to demand an end to British rule. Later Hoda Sharaawi and other well-known feminists symbolically removed their facial veils as part of a campaign to increase the opportunities for women in public affairs. Feminist organizations have been a persistent presence in national life, agitating for educational and social reform and being instrumental in winning suffrage for women in 1956 and constitutional equality in 1962.

It would be a mistake to view the young women of Egypt today who have been inspired by Islam as breaking substantively with the past. They are, instead, simply taking advantage of widening educational opportunities and involving themselves in Egyptian daily life on a scale that is unprecedented.

Young women who have been inspired by Islam are taking advantage of educational opportunities and becoming involved in Egyptian daily life on an unprecedented scale.

The Egyptian Political Scene

The Nasser Period. When the Free Officers, led by Lt. Col. Gamal Abdel Nasser, forced the abdication of King Farouq in 1952, nearly two millennia of foreign rule ended and Egypt was proclaimed an independent republic. It is interesting to note that both Anwar Sadat, Nasser's successor, and Hosni Mubarak, who succeeded Sadat, were also members of the Free Officers Movement that unseated the monarchy. So significant was the 1952 coup that each of Egypt's leaders since independence has legitimately been known as a nationalist or patriot.

Nasser did not assume the presidency until 1954, when in the wake of political differences Mohammed Naguib, the first president, appointed and installed by the Free Officers, was ousted. Nasser's nationalization of the Suez Canal within two years of his taking office (in July 1956) resulted in a combined British, French, and Israeli attack on Egypt (and the first Israeli invasion of Sinai) that threatened to interrupt shipping through the canal. The United States and the Soviet Union exerted pressure and the trio withdrew, leaving the Suez Canal firmly in Egyptian hands, with the effect of galvanizing Nasser's political leadership, both in Egypt and in the Arab world.

As Nasser moved to consolidate his power, he suppressed both the left, represented by the Communist Party and other leftist organizations, and the right, the conservative Muslim Brotherhood. In the process he forged a political movement based upon popular Arab socialism, using the vehicle of a newly created, single lawful party, the Arab Socialist Union (ASU). The

Gamal Abdel Nasser, first elected president of independent Egypt, held office from 1954 until his death in 1970.

ASU with Nasser at the helm engaged in extensive land reform, and made great strides toward universal, free education and government-sponsored health care. Ultimately, these changes made Nasser a beloved ally of the poor peasant and the urban working class. Many wealthy Egyptians and large landowners left Egypt at this time and settled in Europe, the United States, and Canada, while Egypt built closer ties with the Soviet Union.

Arab socialism expanded to Arab nationalism, with the goal of political unity of the Arab people, and to this end Egypt entered into a union with Syria in 1958 to form the United Arab Republic. This relationship lasted only until 1961, when Syria withdrew after a military coup changed its policies. However, Egypt continued to call itself the United Arab Republic until 1971 (a year after the death of Nasser), when it changed its name to the Arab Republic of Egypt, which it retains to this day.

Egyptians who loved Nasser will say that it was the 1967 war with Israel, when the Sinai Peninsula, the West Bank, Gaza Strip, and Golan Heights were annexed by Israel, that broke Nasser's heart and ultimately killed him (he died of a heart attack on September 28, 1970). Egypt's humiliating defeat appeared to undermine the dream and the very fabric of both Arab socialism and Arab nationalism. Tiny Israel appeared invincible in the face of the vast Arab nation and its armies.

With Nasser's death, the entire Arab world grieved openly, as much for the loss of the ideas associated with the man as for the man himself. Five million people were estimated to have crowded onto Cairo's streets for the funeral procession. Months later, when I visited Egypt for the first time, the mosques and public buildings were still draped in black, memorializing the dead hero.

The Sadat Period. Given the outpouring of sentiment at Nasser's death, the succession of Anwar Sadat was an unheralded event and little was expected of this minor political figure. Although Sadat pledged to continue Nasser's policies, in fact he began to turn, almost immediately, away from Arab socialism and the Soviet Union. Instead of implementing a planned merger with Libya and the Sudan (led by Nasser-styled coup leaders, Moammer Gaddafi and Jaafar Numieri, who constructed their own versions of the single-party Arab Socialist Union), Sadat moved to build better relations with Saudi Arabia, the oil-rich Arab nations, and the United States. He gradually moved to deconstruct the ASU and replaced it in 1978 with his own National Democratic Party (NDP), while allowing a few other political parties to operate openly in a new "democratic" Egypt.

These bold breaks with Nasser's policies were made possible by Sadat's stunning surprise attack on Israel on October 6, 1973, referred to by Egypt as the "10th of Ramadan"[2] war and by Israel as the "Yom Kippur" war. A more neutral reference commonly used in the West is the "October War." Sadat's remarkable crossing of the canal regained an Egyptian foothold in the lost Sinai and, with the subsequent truce, returned the lucrative Suez Canal to Egypt (currently earning close to one billion dollars per year in revenues). The 1979 peace treaty with Israel restored to Egypt the entire Sinai Peninsula with its rich oil fields.

The historic trip by Sadat to Jerusalem in 1977

2. Ramadan is the holy month of fasting in Islam.

marked the first visit by an Arab leader to the state of Israel since its creation in 1948. The strategy was accepted domestically because the war-weary Egyptians were anxious for peace, and because Egypt's military success against Israel in 1973 had salvaged its national dignity. Egyptians were tired, many said, of shouldering alone the burden of the Arab struggle against Israel, and many supported the separate peace with Israel that was at the foundation of the 1978 Camp David Accords. They believed that Egyptian victories engineered by Sadat in the 1973 war were responsible for bringing Israel to the negotiating table at Camp David. Others raised the question, "Peace at what price?" since the concessions made by Sadat, they argued, were excessive. They were skeptical of a purportedly comprehensive and lasting peace plan that did not include such major parties to the Mid East conflict as the Palestinians, Syrians, and Jordanians, who had also been at war with Israel. Although high drama surrounded the meeting at Camp David of Jimmy Carter, Anwar Sadat, and Menachem Begin (the latter two sharing the 1978 Nobel Peace Prize), the major gain achieved by Egypt, besides the mutual peace agreement, was a withdrawal date of April 25, 1982, for the Israelis' full return of Sinai.

The separate peace with Israel was exacted at a great price with respect to Egypt's position in the Arab world. Peace with Israel and the subsequent establishment of diplomatic relations meant the utter isolation of Egypt and a precipitous fall from its prominent position as leader of the Arab world. In practical terms Arab aid, which had constituted about three billion dollars annually in direct assistance, loans, and credit, was suspended, and the United States stepped in to fill the vacuum at two and a half billion dollars annually.

At the conclusion of the Camp David Summit in 1978, President Anwar Sadat (left), President Carter, and Israeli Prime Minister Menachem Begin signed two agreements providing for negotiation of a Middle East peace treaty.

With over three billion dollars in U.S. aid allocated to Israel's three million inhabitants and two and a half billion dollars allotted to Egypt's population of forty-five million people, the inevitable comparisons have been made throughout the Middle East, and the inevitable questions continue to be asked regarding favoritism and equitable treatment. The high cost of this fragile peace is an issue, and one might ask if peace has been achieved at all.

With the October 6, 1981, assassination of Sadat by an underground Islamic fundamentalist group, both

Sadat's isolation from the Egyptian people that had developed in the years since Camp David and Egypt's isolation from the rest of the Arab world became painfully apparent. Although a popular leader in the West, Sadat had grown increasingly repressive and corrupt at home, and his funeral, unlike that of Nasser only a decade earlier, attracted little public participation and was even an occasion for rejoicing in parts of the Arab world. A year after his assassination when I was living in Cairo, I attempted, without success, to purchase a picture of Sadat. Unlike Nasser's portrait, which is still proudly displayed in stores and other public places, photographs of Sadat are conspicuously absent.

The Hosni Mubarak Period. Sadat's successor, Hosni Mubarak, had been vice-president since 1975 and was widely viewed as a loyalist who would make no substantive breaks with Sadat's policies. That forecast has proven to be accurate for the most part. He has, for example, presided over the return of Sinai to Egypt from Israel. However, since the death of Sadat, Islamic forces have grown dramatically and Mubarak has had to respond positively to them without using repressive force. He has had to accept the legitimacy of Islamic alternatives to Egypt's nearly four decades of secular, military rule on the one hand, while condemning Islamic extremists' acts of violence on the other. Parliamentary elections in 1987 returned a majority of Mubarak's backers to the People's Assembly, but a significant 20 percent of the vote went to candidates backed by the Islamic forces. In summary, Mubarak appears to have temporarily succeeded in recognizing the growing strength of the Islamic forces by bringing them into the political process. This policy is essential because the Islamic movements represent the most

Current president of Egypt, Hosni Mubarak, succeeded Anwar Sadat after the latter's assasination in 1981.

recent and challenging dynamic in Egyptian society today.

Relations with the United States. During most of Nasser's tenure, Egypt was allied with the Soviet Union. Upon Nasser's death, Sadat opened the door for relations with the West. From the United States' defense of Egypt's right to control the Suez Canal in 1956 to the Camp David initiative by President Jimmy Carter in 1978, Egypt has, from time to time, perceived the United States as its friend and ally. However, America's seemingly unconditional support for Israel has often left Egypt feeling like a poor country cousin with respect to the dominant concerns of the United States in the Middle East.

With Sadat's assassination in 1981, many in the United States and in Israel feared for the future of the Camp David Accords. However, except for recalling the Egyptian ambassador from Israel during the latter's 1982 invasion of Lebanon, Mubarak has done little to distance himself from the policies put into place by his predecessor.

Since its independence, Egypt has been ruled only by secular, military governments that have not brought lasting peace or economic prosperity to the country. Its future relationships with the United States and with Israel depend on whether Egyptians continue this course or adopt a new one, most probably along more Islamic lines.

The Government, the Press, and Egyptian Humor. The Egyptian republic is headed by an elected president with an appointed vice-president, prime minister, cabinet ministers, and twenty-four governors of Egypt's provinces. The People's Assembly, a feature of political life since the deconstruction of Nasser's Arab Socialist Union, is an elective body dominated by the party of the president, but it has increasingly provided a forum for opposition voices and parties. Although, theoretically, this structure represents a power-sharing arrangement, the presidency, with its powerful connection with the army, has held a dominant place in Egyptian politics. Since the constitution that was enacted in the early days of Sadat, executive authority rests with the president who is also chief of state and supreme commander of the armed forces. Presidents are elected by a popular referendum, but typically run unopposed.

There is no official press, but certain major newspapers, like *Al-Ahram,* are semiofficial government outlets. Depending upon domestic security conditions, the opposition newspapers flourish and are eagerly awaited on their regular days of issue.

Egyptian political humor, indeed the ability of the people to make light of many of life's great and small trials, is a widely admired feature of Egyptian culture. Within days of the devastating 1967 war, the most serious blow to Egyptian national pride in recent times, jokes about the war and the bravery of the Egyptian army were circulating widely throughout the country. Frequently, expatriates inquire about life back home in Egypt by asking for a recitation of the latest jokes. Sociologists and political scientists analyze this phenomenon as a means of social catharsis, whereas the Egyptians simply relish political, social, and economic humor.

The Egyptian people's ability to look at life with humor is just one of the many inner strengths that have contributed to their ability to withstand foreign occupation and yet maintain a uniquely Egyptian

Political cartoons appear daily in Egypt's newspapers. This one, which is adapted, with English translation, appeared in the May 11, 1983, issue of Al Ahali.

identity. The strength and continuity of Egyptian culture, demonstrated by its endurance and adaptability throughout the millennia—from Pharaonic to Arab-Islamic and later colonial European influences—are Egypt's signal achievements and, together, are the source of the country's richest contribution to world civilization.

Suggested Reading

Abu-Lughod, Janet. *Cairo, 1001 Years of the City Victorious*, Princeton: Princeton University Press, 1971.

Ayrout, Henry Habib. *The Egyptian Peasant.* Boston: Beacon Press, 1978.

Critchfield, Richard. *Shahhat, an Egyptian.* Cairo: The American University in Cairo Press, 1982.

James, T.G.H. *An Introduction to Ancient Egypt.* New York: Farrar Straus Giroux, 1979.

Rugh, Andrea. *Family Life in Contemporary Egypt.* Syracuse: Syracuse University Press, 1984.

Acknowledgments

Photographs and illustrations have come from the following sources and are used by permission:

Front cover: Drawing by Linda A. Witt of panel selected from the catalogue of the "Unity of Islamic Art" Exhibition held at King Faisal Center for Research and Islamic Studies, Riyadh, Saudi Arabia, in 1985
Pp. 3, 5, 14, 15, 19, 21, 28: The Carnegie Museum of Natural History
P. 7: The Carnegie Library of Pittsburgh
Pp. 9, 10: Drawing and map by N.J. Perkins
Pp. 11, 18, 22, 25, 26: Carolyn Fluehr-Lobban
P. 13: Courtesy of D.C. Patch and J.F. Romano; photograph by M. McNaugher
Pp. 30, 36: United Nations
P. 34: UPI/Bettmann Newsphotos
P. 39: Drawing by Patte Kelley